Irish Shrines & Reliquaries of the Middle Ages

Raghnall Ó Floinn

Country House, Dublin
in association wit
The National Museum c

Published in 1994 by
Town House and Country House
42 Morehampton Road
Donnybrook
Dublin 4
Ireland

in association with The National Museum of Ireland

British Library Cataloguing in Publication Data. A catalogue record for this book is available from the British Library.

ISBN: 0-946172-40-4

Acknowledgements
The author and publishers would like to thank the following for permission to reproduce their photographs: Office of Public Works (Photos 14, 18, Pl 8); Trustees of the National Library of Ireland (Photo 7, Pl 1); Board of Trinity College Dublin (Photos 4, 6, 20, Pl 6); Ulster Museum, Belfast (Photo 2); Trustees of the British Museum (Photo 16, Pls 16, 17); Council of the Royal Society of Antiquaries of Ireland (Photos 3, 25); Bord Fáilte (Plate 9); Monaghan County Museum (Pl 15). The remaining photographs are by Valerie Dowling of the National Museum of Ireland.

Design: Bill Murphy
Colour origination: The Kulor Centre
Printed in Ireland by Criterion Press, Dublin

CONTENTS

The cult of the dead, belief in an afterlife and the placing of the remains of persons of importance in shrines, are features of many world religions. The earliest centres of the cult of relics among Christians were in the Mediterranean, and especially the Holy Land. In Rome, the remains of the early Christians buried in the catacombs became subjects of devotion, and services were held at their tombs (Pl 1). Soon, however, these remains were disinterred, divided up, placed in protective reliquaries and carried all over the Christian world. This in turn led to the veneration and enshrining of the relics of local saints and martyrs. The demand for these became so great that objects associated with these holy people, including *brandea* (pieces of cloth that had touched the sacred remains) came to be regarded as sacred in their own right and worthy of enshrinement (Photo 1).

THE CULT OF RELICS IN IRELAND

The use of relics in Ireland dates to the introduction of Christianity, the earliest recorded being those of the early martyrs and saints of the continental Church. Palladius, the first named Christian missionary to Ireland, who arrived in 431, brought with him relics of the apostles Peter and Paul, and of other saints, which were later kept in a box or casket at the Church of Cell Fine, thought to be the site known today as Killeen Cormac, Co Kildare. By the early seventh century, St Patrick's Church at Armagh had acquired relics of the early saints and martyrs, and had begun to distribute these to other churches. These early relics were in short supply and were highly prized. The earliest datable Irish reliquary, found recently at Clonmore, Co Armagh, is just 8cm (3in) long — ideally suited to contain the

Photo 1. Small silver reliquary, measuring just 2cm (¾in), containing a wreath of plaited rush wrapped in linen, found at Straidcayle, Co Antrim. Possibly a personal reliquary, it dates to the late twelfth century and is of English or north German manufacture.

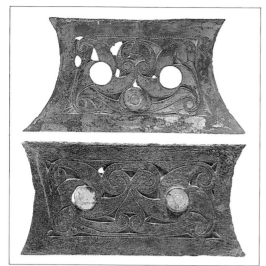

Photo 2. Fragments of a tomb-shaped shrine of tinned bronze from the River Blackwater at Clonmore, Co Armagh. It measures just 8cm (3in) in length and is the earliest datable Irish reliquary.

minute fragments of these valuable continental relics (Photo 2).

As happened elsewhere, within a few centuries of the introduction of Christianity to Ireland, the cult of relics of native Irish saints was under way. Exactly when this occurred we cannot say, but by the middle of the seventh century a text written at Armagh laid down the fines payable for violating or insulting the 'insignia' of Patrick. These must have been objects associated with the saint, perhaps even including one of the numerous bells that in later centuries were linked with him.

The sale and theft of relics was a natural consequence of their popularity. Relic collectors were known in Ireland, such as the eleventh-century poet Onchú, who was based in the monastery of Clonmore, Co Carlow. The ninth-century Life of St Abban records how the monks of the monastery of Killaban, Co Laois, Abban's birthplace, stole his body from the monastery where he died, Magh Arnuidhe (Adamstown, Co Wexford).

By the time of the Viking incursions, references to the destruction of relics are numerous. In 798 the island of Ireland's Eye off the Dublin coast was raided and the Shrine of St Dochonna was broken up. This did not interrupt the practice of enshrining relics, however, as in the year 801 it is recorded that the relics of Ronan, patron saint of Dromiskin, Co Louth,

Photo 3. A stone reliquary with sliding lid, with an inner wooden box which contained the shank of a bronze key, found at Dromiskin, Co Louth. The key — a symbol of St Peter — may have been regarded as a relic of that saint.

were placed in a shrine of gold and silver. Excavations in the last century of the graveyard at Dromiskin revealed a stone-lined grave containing another early reliquary. This consisted of a rectangular stone box with sliding lid, inside of which was a smaller wooden box of similar construction. Within this was a bronze object, thought to be the key of a small padlock (Photo 3). What

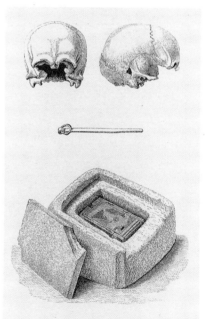

this object signified is a mystery, but it was obviously of sufficient importance to be worthy of enshrinement.

In common with continental Europe, during the eleventh and twelfth centuries a number of Irish saints' remains were exhumed and placed in ornamented shrines or reliquaries. These included the remains of St Colman of Lann (Lynn, Co Westmeath), St Comman of Roscommon, St Manchan of Mohill, Co Leitrim, and Saints Maeineann and Cummaine Foda at Clonfert, Co Galway. It is no coincidence that a large number of Irish reliquaries can be dated to this time. This was a period of great change in Irish society. The organisation and structure of the Church was undergoing radical reform, and at the same time political power was being concentrated among a small group of dynasties who had ambitions to overall control of the island. The diocesan structure was established in a series of synods, and associations with a particular saint and the possession of his/her relics would have been an important asset to any church competing with its neighbour for diocesan status and secular patronage. An example of this is the monastery of Roscrea, Co Tipperary, where within a short period in the twelfth century, a Gospel book associated with its patron saint, Crónán, was enshrined (the so-called Shrine of the Book of Dimma — Photo 4), a Life of the saint was composed, a new

Photo 4. Shrine of the Book of Dimma, associated with Roscrea, Co Tipperary. Originally made in the twelfth century, it was repaired in the mid fourteenth century by an O'Carroll, king of Éile.

church in the Romanesque style was built, and at least one high cross was erected. Although unsuccessful in pursuit of its claim to diocesan status in 1111, the monastery was finally established as such at the Synod of Kells in 1152. The same pattern of artistic patronage was repeated at many Irish monastic centres, resulting in the enshrinement of relics, the composition of saints' Lives and the construction of monuments such as churches, crosses and round towers.

The Anglo-Normans, who were familiar with the concept, realised the importance of the cult of relics of native Irish saints in maintaining control over the areas they colonised. John de Courcy, who conquered Ulster, captured a collection of relics and their shrines at the Battle of Downpatrick in 1177, including several croziers and two bells associated with Armagh, some of which were returned by him shortly afterwards (Pl 2). He arranged for the bodies of the three principal Irish saints, Patrick, Brigid and Colmcille, to be miraculously discovered and enshrined at Downpatrick in 1185, encouraged devotion to St Patrick, and was patron to Jocelin of Furness, who wrote the first Anglo-Norman Life of the saint. All this was designed to garner support among the Irish. The spurious nature of the 1185 translation is shown by the record of the discovery of the remains of the same three saints in 1293 at Saul, Co Down, by Nicholas Mac Mael Íosa, Archbishop of Armagh. This confusion is bound up with the fact that the resting place of Patrick was disputed and that Armagh could never claim to be his resting place.

During the later Middle Ages, there is further evidence for the use of relics for political ends. A number have survived from the fourteenth and fifteenth centuries that can be linked to prominent Irish families, who saw the decline in the fortunes of the English administration as a chance to re-establish older claims to kingship. Thus Art Mac Murrough Kavanagh, claimant to the title of King of Leinster, had a new shrine made in 1403 for an ancient Gospel book associated with the monastery of St Mullins, Co Carlow. In Munster in the 1370s, Phillip O'Kennedy, King of Ormond, had a new cover made for the Shrine of the Stowe Missal. Some of the established Anglo-Norman families who had adopted Irish customs and laws were also engaged in similar work. Thomas de Bermingham, Lord of Athenry, Co Galway, commissioned a radical alteration of an early twelfth-century object known as the Shrine of St Patrick's Tooth (Pl 3). This work was done about the same time as the work on the Stowe Missal Shrine, and may even have been undertaken by the same person (Photo 5).

Book and bell shrines continued to be redecorated or made anew well into the sixteenth century. Two book shrines, the Shrine of St Caillinn of Fenagh, Co Leitrim, bearing the names of its patrons, Brian O'Rourke and his wife Margaret, and the date 1526, and the shrine known as the Miosach, dated 1534 (Pl 4), are structurally almost identical to the book shrines of the eighth century. This is largely because the craftworkers repairing the shrines replicated many of their features. Many other reliquaries show evidence of less competent work, usually in

the form of pieces of rock crystal mounted in settings of coarse silver filigree.

The impact of the Reformation was greatest in the towns and in areas under direct English control, and it was here that the greatest destruction of relics and sacred images took place. Consequently, virtually all the surviving relics of the later Middle Ages are from the north and west of Ireland. Yet we know from the inventory of objects in the treasury of Christ Church Cathedral in Dublin and from other documents that the churches and abbeys of the larger towns were well-endowed (Photo 6). The head reliquary of St Patrick, preserved in the Hunt Collection, Limerick, is a unique example of the type of reliquary that one would expect to see in a late medieval town. Its inscription states that it was made for James Butler, Earl of Ormond and Justiciar of Ireland, in honour of St Patrick. It is not possible to identify the exact patron of this remarkable piece, but the fourth or 'White' Earl who died in 1452 has been suggested.

Relics of Irish saints continued to be made in the seventeenth and eighteenth centuries, and indeed continue to be refurbished down to the present day. Many of the older relics were recorded in the early nineteenth century as being used at patterns (a patron saint's day), fairs and other gatherings, where they were hired out for use as cures and for swearing oaths (Photo 7). By the time of the disestablishment of the Church of Ireland and Catholic Emancipation in the

Photo 5. Details from (a) the Shrine of the Stowe Missal and (b) the Shrine of St Patrick's Tooth, both of mid-fourteenth-century date. The style of engraving on both is so close that they may be the work of the one craftsman — Domhnall Ó Tolairi — whose name is inscribed on the book shrine.

Photo 6. List of relics preserved at Christ Church Cathedral, Dublin, in the fifteenth century. The list includes the miracle-working 'speaking crucifix' of Dublin, as well as relics of St Patrick and other Irish and continental saints.

Photo 7. Pattern day at a holy well, c.1840. Relics were often brought by their keepers to such gatherings, and cures were offered for a small consideration. Note the hawker selling rosary beads, the rag-bush behind him, and the holy water being collected in bottles.

1830s, it appears that the use of such objects was discouraged as part of the attempts by the Catholic Church to stamp out superstitious practices associated with relics and holy wells.

THE USE OF RELICS

The uses to which relics and reliquaries were put in the medieval period are amply documented in the written sources, particularly in the Lives of the saints. The earliest of these date to the seventh century, but most date to the eleventh and twelfth centuries, the same period as the majority of the surviving reliquaries. The majority of relics, at least of those that survive today, were designed to be carried about. As a result, they were liable to much wear, damage and even loss, often requiring frequent repairs. This is one of the main reasons why the individual reliquaries in our museums show evidence of workmanship of several different periods.

The practice of bringing relics on circuit to promulgate the 'laws' of a particular saint goes back to the seventh century (Pl 5). In this way, dependent churches were bound to the main foundation, ecclesiastical laws were enforced, taxes levied and tribute (gifts, etc) collected. In the case of Armagh, for instance, the 'law' of Patrick was promulgated in Connacht in 783, 799 and 825, and in Munster in 823 and 842. In each case, the relics of the saint probably accompanied the Armagh clerics on their circuits. On other occasions, it appears that the circuit of relics may have followed natural disasters such as plagues or bad weather, for example, the outbreak of smallpox in 742–43 coincided with the circuit of the relics of Kildalkey, Co Meath.

The belief in the power of relics to effect miraculous cures is an equally early custom and is frequently mentioned in the Lives of the saints (Photos 8, 9). The belts or girdles of saints were considered particularly effective, especially in relation to problems of childbirth. Water drunk from a holy bell could cure a variety of ailments, from boils to poor hearing. The use of relics for their curative powers was to be their most enduring function, and one that was almost universally noted by nineteenth-century observers. The best known example is perhaps the seventeenth-century account of how the Book of Durrow was steeped in water which was

Photo 8. The shrine known as the Corp Naomh (Holy Body). Formerly preserved at Templecross, Co Westmeath, it was described in 1682 as 'held to this day in great veneration by all of the Romish persuasion that live hereabouts; on occasion it is offered to them as a sacred oath, by which none dare swear falsely'.

Photo 9. Reliquary found in 1945 in a bog at Moylough, Co Sligo. Made of four decorated hinged plates, each enclosing a piece of leather, presumably the sacred girdle of an unknown saint. It dates to the eighth century.

subsequently used as a cure for sick cattle (Pl 6).

Relics were also objects on which oaths were sworn, and were regarded as the guarantors of compacts and treaties. In some cases, depending on the importance of the treaty, large numbers of relics were produced on both sides to act as symbolic witnesses. Of these, the most frequently cited is the Bachall Íosa, the great staff of Saint Patrick, probably the most important Irish reliquary of the medieval period. This practice, noted by Gerald of Wales in the twelfth century, was also to persist well into the nineteenth century. The antiquary George Petrie recounts a case in Sligo in 1835 where a court case was postponed until the shrine known as the Soiscéal Molaise was produced, as one party objected to swearing on the Bible.

The use of relics as battle talismans is well documented. Being possessed of supernatural powers, their presence on the battlefield would ensure victory. The best known example is the enshrined manuscript known as the Cathach, associated with St Colmcille, which was the battle standard of the O'Donnells (Photo 10). Elsewhere croziers and trumpets are noted as talismans.

Photo 10. Back of the Shrine of the Cathach, bearing an openwork design of pierced crosses. The inscription around the edge shows that the work was carried out at the monastery of Kells, Co Meath, in the late eleventh century.

The practice of cursing one's enemies in order to bring bad luck is a motif found in the earliest saints' Lives. By ringing a bell or making the Sign of the Cross with a crozier, ill-fortune and even death could be willed upon the miscreant. The penalty of death was usually reserved for those who plundered or raided monasteries. The Lives of the saints were not simply biographies, but were often written with a particular political purpose in mind.

Episodes relating to relics were sometimes included to explain their presence in a particular church (Photo 11). The miracles wrought by a saint using his bell or crozier during his life, or even after his death, were recounted in order to encourage pilgrimage, thereby enhancing the status and income of his foundation. The possession of relics by a church or monastery served to increase its status and wealth. Relics ensured special protection to the community and also attracted pilgrims — a valuable source of income.

Photo 11. Detail from the Domhnach Airgid shrine, illustrating an episode from the Life of St Patrick in which the saint, seated left, presents the relic — a book — to St Mac Cairthinn, patron saint of Clones, Co Monaghan.

In Ireland, some monasteries were grouped into 'families', sharing a common founding saint. The monastery that claimed primacy over the federation was in possession of that saint's relics, and the distribution of these to other foundations symbolised the common ties between the churches.

Thus the importance of relics goes beyond the purely symbolic and devotional, and the enshrining of relics was often as much a political statement as an act of piety. The reasons for enshrining the relics are often related to specific events associated with a particular church or monastery, occasioned by, perhaps, a new patron or by rivalries between communities. The provision of a new shrine often coincided with the construction of a new church and other monuments, or the composition of a new Life of a saint, which sometimes sought to explain how the relics were obtained.

Many of these themes are illustrated in the Life of St Flannan of Killaloe, Co Clare. St Flannan was the most important Clare saint, and although no relic associated with him survives today, the Life of the saint, written probably at Killaloe at the end of the twelfth century, contains important details of his relics, which were in existence at that time. The Life also chronicles the rise in importance of Killaloe as a centre of pilgrimage due to the miraculous powers of his relics. After Flannan's death, his sanctity attracted crowds to his tomb where, through his intercession, miracles were said to have taken place. Eventually, in order to accommodate the ever-increasing number of pilgrims, permission was granted by the Pope to disinter his body and place it in a shrine where it could be more easily venerated. The local chiefs contributed a vast amount of silver and gold for the elaborate shrine.

This episode in the Life of St Flannan is a typical example of a *translatio*, that is, the disinterment of the body of a saint from its original resting place and its removal to a new position of honour. In this case, the sacred objects used by the saint — his book, bell and crozier — were also enshrined. We are not told when these events occurred, but the Life was compiled under the patronage of the O'Briens in the late twelfth century, and it is likely that the relics were enshrined sometime during the eleventh or twelfth centuries, when the O'Briens dominated the ecclesiastical politics of Killaloe.

TYPES OF RELICS

The surviving Irish relics may be divided into two types: corporeal relics, that is, parts of the bodies of holy people, and associative relics, consisting of objects used by or associated with a saint during his or her lifetime.

Corporeal relics
Corporeal relics were obtained by exhuming or 'translating' the body of a saint from its original resting place. In the Mediterranean world the tombs of these holy people often consisted of stone sarcophagi built above ground. The earliest forms of reliquary known from Ireland have been given the misleading name 'house-shaped shrines', but in fact they have nothing to do with contemporary Irish architecture. More properly called 'tomb-shaped reliquaries', they are versions of a common European type, and their contents and proportions indicate that they are miniature versions of Late Antique sarcophagi. Surviving Irish examples range in date from the later sixth to the tenth centuries (Photo 2, Pl 7). Some are composed entirely of metal while others have a wooden core. They usually have a hinged lid to allow access to the relics, with hinge attachments to enable them to be carried around the neck on straps. The earliest examples are also the smallest, the increased size of the later examples reflecting the more plentiful supply of relics with the passing of time. They were made using separate metal plates for each side, and held together at the edges with binding strips formed of split tubes of metal, kept in place by nails. This simple constructional technique was to be used for the next thousand years with little variation for other types of reliquary, particularly bell and book shrines.

There is evidence to suggest that the earlier tomb-shaped reliquaries were designed not for the relics of Irish saints but to hold the precious relics of the continental saints and martyrs of the early Church. Although no Irish reliquary of this type still retains its original contents, comparable examples on the Continent suggest that the form was reserved for keeping corporeal relics.

A number of these tomb-shaped reliquaries are known from Viking graves in Norway, appropriated for use as jewellery caskets. Such an episode is recorded in 824 when the Vikings invaded Bangor, Co Down, 'and the relics of Comgall

[Bangor's founding saint] were shaken out of their shrine'. More examples of the type are now being recognised in museums and church treasuries in Italy, Belgium and France, and are eloquent physical testimonies of the missionary activities of Irish monks.

Like their Mediterranean counterparts, the early graves or tomb shrines of Irish saints were invariably built above ground (Pls 8, 9). Erected outdoors, they were composed of stone slabs arranged in the manner of a gabled roof, or box-shaped, often with grooved corner posts which betray their origins as wooden structures. Very few have been securely dated, but their origins must lie ultimately with the same Late Antique sarcophagi that inspired the tomb-shaped reliquaries. Some were provided with a hole through which the pilgrim could touch the sacred bones.

A second type of tomb-shaped reliquary designed to take the complete remains of a saint was also known. Made of wood covered with metal plates, these were accorded a position of honour, being placed on or beside the high altar. We know from the seventh-century Life of St Brigid of Kildare that two such reliquaries 'adorned with a refined profusion of gold, silver, gems and precious stones' containing the bodies of Archbishop Conlaed and St Brigid, flanked the main altar of the church at Kildare. No large shrine of this type survives, but the gilt bronze 'butterfly finials' (gable or roof ornaments) of unknown provenance preserved in the Musée Nationale at St Germain, near Paris, may originally have been fitted to the crest of such a large gabled shrine (Photo 12).

Photo 12. Pair of mounts preserved at St Germain, near Paris, France. They were originally attached to the gable end of a large tomb shrine. Fragments of very similar mounts, perhaps from the same shrine, are known from a Viking grave in Norway.

Photo 13. Shrine of St
Manchan, preserved at
Boher Church, Co
Offaly, dating to the
early twelfth century.
The largest surviving
Irish reliquary, it still
contains human bones,
believed to be relics of
the saint.

An early, perhaps eighth-century example of a gabled tomb-shaped reliquary was preserved in a church in north Wales in the seventeenth century; made of wood covered with metal mounts, it contained the relics of St Winifred. The only surviving Irish example is St Manchan's Shrine, which dates to the twelfth century (Photo 13). This is preserved in the parish church of Boher, Co Offaly, not far from its original home, the monastery of Lemanaghan. It constitutes the largest and most impressive Irish reliquary, measuring some 60cm (24in) in length and 50cm (20in) in height. Now sadly mutilated, it is decorated on each main face with an elaborate bossed metal cross, and one face retains some of the cast human figures (apostles and saints?) that adorned both sides. Resting on four feet, it has rings at each corner to enable it to be mounted on two carrying poles. Remarkably, it still contains some human bones.

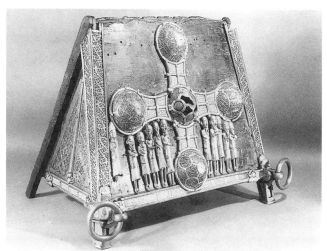

The Crusades were responsible for bringing back relics and reliquaries from the eastern Church, which were to influence western ideas. One of these new forms appears to have been the arm reliquary, and the object known as the Shrine of St Lachtin's Arm, dated by its inscription to c.1120, is among the earliest western examples (Pl 10). It is unique in that it depicts a closed fist, and the interlaced decoration of the hand suggests a patterned glove. In form it is closer to contemporary Byzantine than to western European examples. Its appearance in Ireland at such an early date indicates how much in touch the Irish Church was with contemporary European developments. Other arm reliquaries are known to have existed at Lorrha, Co Tipperary, and Clonmacnoise, Co Offaly, as late as the seventeenth century, but the only other extant Irish example is the fifteenth-century Shrine of St Patrick's Hand, now in the Ulster Museum, Belfast.

The general absence of corporeal relics in Ireland calls for special comment. None of the early Irish tomb-shaped reliquaries can be shown to have been preserved above ground, in fact most have been recovered from rivers and lakes. They also lack inscriptions. As a result, their early history, especially the churches and saints with which they were associated, is unknown. At the same time few corporeal relics have survived from later times. This can in part be explained by the fact that large reliquaries of any kind (such as those designed to hold the entire body of a saint) are unlikely to have survived the medieval period in an intact state,

cont. p 33

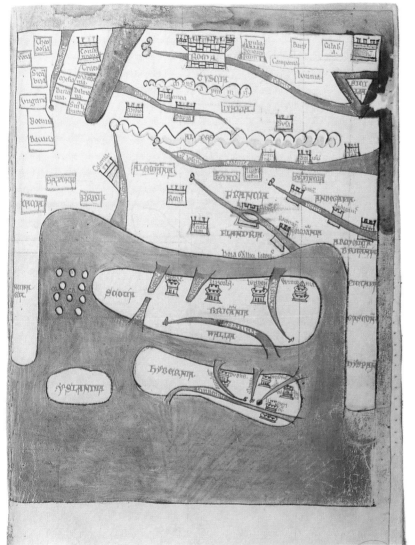

*Pl 1. Map of Europe,
from* Topography of
Ireland *by Giraldus
Cambrensis, dating to
around the year 1200.
Ireland is at the
bottom, Norway to the
left and Spain to the
right. The map seems to
show the pilgrim's route
to Rome, which is at
the top centre.*

Pl 2. St Patrick's Bell (a) and its shrine (b). The poor condition of the front of the shrine is explained by the fact that pieces of it were removed in the last century 'to be used as charms against disease and other evils'.

a

b

Pl 3. The Shrine of St Patrick's Tooth. This twelfth-century reliquary was substantially repaired in the mid fourteenth century for Thomas de Bermingham, Lord of Athenry. When opened in the last century, it was found to contain pieces of cloth and a small lead cross.

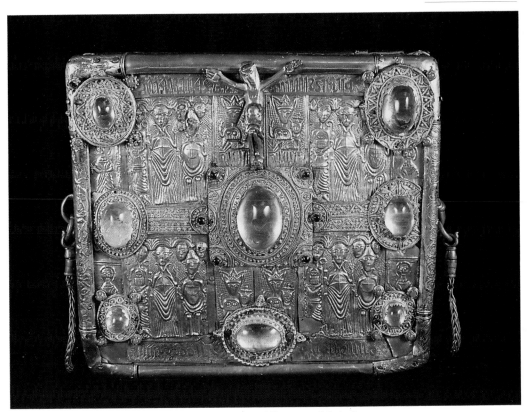

Pl 4. Shrine known as the Miosach. The older parts date to the twelfth century, while the front was redecorated in 1534. Although its contents are now missing, its shape suggests that it functioned as a book shrine.

Pl 5. Drawing of c.1640 showing the abbot of Holycross Abbey on horseback carrying the relic of the True Cross on circuit. He is preceded by a retainer carrying a banner on which the Cross is depicted. The relic was kept in a bag hung around his neck (see Photo 22, a & b).

Pl 6. (Facing page) The Book of Durrow, dating to the seventh century. In the later Middle Ages, the manuscript was dipped in water, which was used as a cure for sick cattle. Note the holes in the vellum caused by the resulting dampness.

7

8

Pl 9. Twelfth-century tomb shrine at Clones, Co Monaghan. Note the 'butterfly finials' at each end of the roof ridge. The St Germain finials (Photo 12) would have belonged to a shrine of similar size, made of wood covered with decorated metal plates.

Pl 7. (Facing page) Two tomb-shaped shrines from Lough Erne, Co Fermanagh, which were found entangled in a fishing line. The smaller shrine was placed inside the larger.

Pl 8. (Facing page) The church of Temple Cronan in the Burren, Co Clare, with a gable-shaped slab shrine in the foreground, similar in shape to St Manchan's shrine (Photo 13).

*Pl 10. Shrine of St
Lachtin's Arm,
Donaghmore, Co Cork,
dated by a series of
inscriptions to between
1118 and 1121. The
metal plates are
attached to a wooden
core, which was
hollowed to receive the
relic — a portion of the
saint's arm bone. The
relic no longer survives.*

*Pl 11. The Lismore
Crozier. Found during
the removal of a
blocked-up doorway at
Lismore Castle, Co
Waterford, it bears the
name of an abbot of
Lismore who died in
1113, as well as the
name of the craftsman,
Nechtan, who made it.*

Pl 12. Shrine known as the Domhnach Airgid. It contained fragments of a gospel book of eighth or ninth-century date. Fragments of wood found behind the front crystal were regarded as relics of the True Cross.

Pl 13. Shrine of the Cathach — the battle standard of the O'Donnell's. The manuscript it contained was thought to have been written by St Colmcille himself. Note the hinged lid, which allows access to the relic.

Pl 14. Watercolour of
the Cross of Cong by
Henry O'Neill, dating
to the 1850s or 60s.
O'Neill was one of the
champions of the Celtic
Revival. Through his
illustrated works on
early Irish art, he
sought to 'show that
Irish civilisation can no
longer be a subject of
doubt'.

Pl 15. The fifteenth-century Cross of Clogher, recovered from a church in Co Fermanagh and now in Monaghan County Museum. The Cross of St Attracta of Killaraght, Co Roscommon, which is mentioned frequently in medieval documents, no longer survives, but it may well have resembled this cross.

Pl 16. (Facing page) Shrine for the Bearnán Conaill bell. Its last keeper, Conal O'Breslen, sold the bell and its shrine c.1833 for three cows and an annuity to a Donegal collector, Major Nesbitt of Ardara. The bell and shrine are now in the British Museum.

Pl 17. Twelfth-century bell shrine with its iron bell, known as the Bearnán Cuileain. Said to have been found inside a hollow tree at Kilcuilawn, near Glankeen, Co Tipperary, it passed into the collection of T L Cooke of Birr, and is now in the British Museum.

Pl 18. Shrine, of about 1100, known as the Breac Maedhóg, along with its leather satchel, some three hundred years later in date. The shrine was kept by its hereditary keepers, the O'Farrellys, at Drumlane, Co Cavan, until purchased by George Petrie in the last century.

cont. from p 16

at a time when the plundering and burning of churches was commonplace and
when only smaller, portable reliquaries were more easily saved. A second reason
may well have been the absence of documented locations of the burial places of the
early Irish saints, epitomised by the disputed resting place of St Patrick. It may well
be that corporeal reliquaries were never very common in the medieval Irish
Church. Certainly in the medieval saints' Lives, the references to the veneration
and enshrining of objects associated with them, whether they be bells, croziers or
books, outnumber by far those references to corporeal remains.

Associative relics

Most of the surviving Irish relics and reliquaries consist of objects believed to have
been associated with the early saints. This also holds true for the Church in pre-
Norman Scotland and, to a lesser extent, Wales, both areas that were influenced by
Irish practices. Although known elsewhere in Europe, relics of this type do not
survive in such proportionately high numbers. This peculiarity was noted by an
early visitor to Ireland, Gerald of Wales. Writing at the end of the twelfth century
he observed, 'I should not omit to mention also that the people and clergy of both
Wales and Ireland have a great reverence for bells that can be carried about, and
staffs belonging to the saints, and made of gold and silver, or bronze, and curved at
their upper ends. So much so that they fear to swear or perjure themselves in
making oaths on these, much more than they do in swearing on the gospels.'

*Photo 14. Detail from
a high cross at Old
Kilcullen, Co Kildare.
It shows a figure
holding a crozier in his
left hand and an axe in
his right. Above and to
the right are a book
and a bell.*

Gerald's description accurately reflects the fact that
the objects most frequently enshrined were croziers or
staffs and hand-bells (Photo 14). Both objects are
frequently depicted on contemporary sculpture and
manuscript paintings and were regarded as the insignia
of office of a cleric. Manuscripts believed to have been
written or used by the early saints were also venerated.
Other objects such as cloaks, belts and shoes were
enshrined, but few of these have survived; the Shrine
of St Brigid's Shoe, once kept at Loughrea, Co
Galway, and the Moylough Belt Shrine, associated
with an unknown saint and found in 1945 in a bog in
Co Sligo, are rare examples (Photos 9, 15, 27).

Many of these objects were not relics when first
used, but acquired their sanctity through contact, or
presumed contact, with a holy person. Thus the
bronze-coated iron bell of St Patrick served as a
functional hand-bell before it was elevated to the status
of a relic through the belief that it was used by the
saint.

15
16

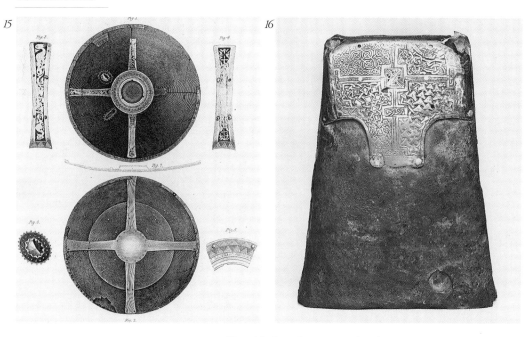

Photo 15. Shrine known as the Mias Tighearnáin or Paten of St Tighearnán of Errew, Co Mayo. Preserved by the O'Flynn family, it dates to the fourteenth or fifteenth centuries.

Photo 16. Iron bell of St Conall of Inishkeel, Co Donegal, known as the Bearnán Conaill. The decorated metal plate was added in the tenth century. Enclosed in its shrine (Pl 16), the bell was venerated by pilgrims visiting the saint's well on his feast day.

Two main types of hand-bell are known, made of iron and bronze respectively. Bells of forged iron dipped in bronze appear to be the older — how much older is hard to tell (Photo 16). Many have been found in graves or in churchyards, suggesting that they were considered of sufficient importance to be buried with prominent churchmen. Reliquaries designed to protect these often consist of hollow boxes composed of decorated bronze sheets, with curved crests to accommodate the handle. The earliest of these date to the ninth century, but most belong to the eleventh and twelfth centuries (Pls 2, 16, 17).

The earliest bells of cast bronze are dated to the early ninth century. Although many of these were regarded as relics, there is no definite evidence that they were enshrined. Some have decoration applied directly to the surface of the bell, but it is not clear if this was an act of enshrinement or purely ornamental.

The other main category of associative relic, the crozier, almost certainly functioned as a pastoral staff or crook (Photo 18). The earliest examples date to the eighth and ninth centuries, and contain all the distinctive characteristics of the Irish crozier — curved crook of horseshoe shape and cast knops or bosses spaced along a fairly short stem. Later croziers, such as that from Lismore, Co Waterford, were provided with cavities for relics (Pl 11). The hollow crest of the Lismore Crozier contains a piece of wood wrapped in a sheet of bronze, while the crook contains a piece of cloth and a small bronze box, inside of which is an unidentified relic (Photo 19). The box with its relic recalls that found at Dromiskin, Co Louth.

cont. p 36

Photo 18. Tomb slab of a bishop, dating to c.1300, at Kilfenora, Co Clare. It shows the figure holding a crozier of Irish type, with raised crest and four barrel-shaped knops.

Photo 19. Relics that were inserted into the Lismore Crozier, consisting of a small box, a sliver of wood and a piece of cloth.

Photo 17. The bell shrine of St Senan of Scattery Island, Co Clare, known as the Clogán Óir (Little Golden Bell). The original bell is missing, but its two outer casings survive. The one shown here is of late eleventh-century date.

cont. from p 34

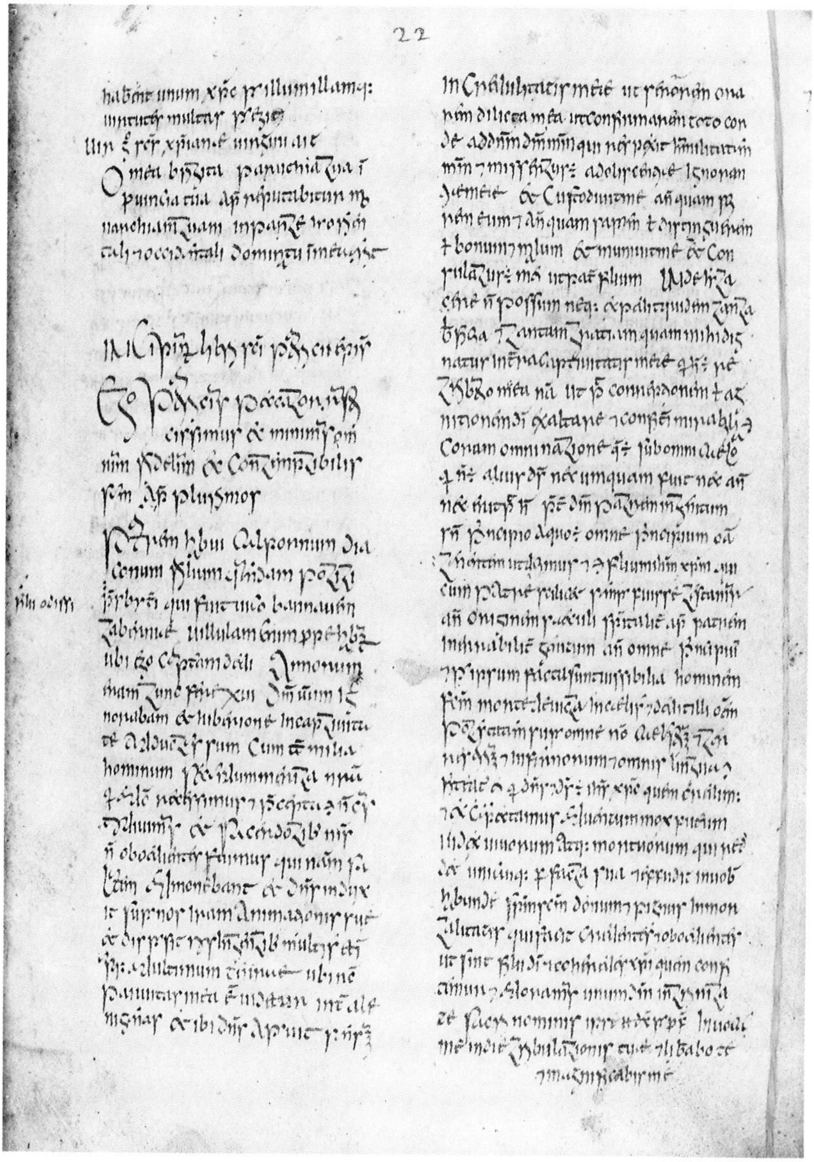

Photo 20. The Book of Armagh, made for Torbach, abbot of Armagh in 807. Apart from the text of the Gospels, it also contains several texts relating to St Patrick, and was therefore regarded as a relic of the saint.

Although we have no evidence that the Lismore Crozier itself was revered as a relic, we do know that many other croziers were.

Manuscripts were enshrined by being placed in boxes, either composed of metal plates or of hollowed pieces of wood to which metal plates were attached (Photos 20, 21; Pls 12, 13). The earliest book shrine is that recently found in a dismantled

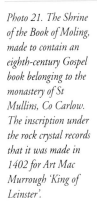

Photo 21. The Shrine of the Book of Moling, made to contain an eighth-century Gospel book belonging to the monastery of St Mullins, Co Carlow. The inscription under the rock crystal records that it was made in 1402 for Art Mac Murrough 'King of Leinster'.

state in Lough Kinale, Co Longford. Dating to the eighth century, its size and sumptuous decoration suggests that it contained a large Gospel book, similar in size to the Book of Kells. Many of these book shrines were designed as sealed containers, making access to their contents difficult.

Without the evidence of written history, we cannot be certain how many of the surviving bells, croziers and manuscripts were regarded as relics.

While some objects were venerated as relics from quite early times, the traditions attached to others are quite late. For example, a bell found in the churchyard of Drumhome, Co Donegal, in 1845 was subsequently given the name 'Bell of Drumhome' or 'St Ernan's Bell', and was used to effect cures in the same way as ancient relics, but the traditions associated with it can only date from the time of its discovery.

Relics of the True Cross are recorded in Ireland from the ninth century (Photos 22, 23). A relic of the True Cross was sent to Ireland by Pope Calixtus II in 1119. Turlough O'Connor, King of Connacht, got permission to retain a portion of it, which was almost certainly enclosed in the Cross of Cong, Co Mayo, made, on the evidence of its inscription, sometime in the 1120s or 30s (Pl 14). Another relic of the True Cross was preserved in the cathedral at Raphoe, Co Donegal, in the later Middle Ages, where it attracted pilgrims from all over Ireland until it was burnt by looting English soldiers in 1600.

Crosses associated with saints were also known (Pl 15). The Great Cross of

Photo 22. a) Relic of the True Cross and b) its silver shrine, preserved at Holycross Abbey, Co Tipperary. The shrine is set with two polished stones, between which is a hinged door that could be opened to view the relic.

Colmcille was preserved on Tory Island, Co Donegal, and the Cross of St Attracta was kept at Elphin, Co Roscommon. A pectoral cross with a relic of St Colmcille was part of the booty taken from Dunluce Castle, a MacDonnell stronghold in Co Antrim, and in 1584 it was sent to Lord Burghley, Queen Elizabeth's Secretary of State, with the request that it be offered to Lady Walsingham or Lady Sydney to wear as a jewel.

INSCRIPTIONS

One interesting aspect of the Irish reliquaries is that a number carry inscriptions naming the people involved in their manufacture. This practice goes back at least to the early tenth century, the earliest known example being the now lost Shrine of the Book of Durrow, which bore on its main face a silver cross engraved with the name of the craftsman who made it, along with the name of Flann Sinna, King of Ireland from 877 to 915. Flann's son, Donnchadh, had a cover made for the Book of Armagh in 937, and although it also no longer survives, it is likely that it too bore an inscription. The earliest extant example is the Soiscéal Molaise book shrine dating to the early eleventh century.

*Photo 23. Cross from
Kilkenny West, Co
Westmeath. Its double-
armed form suggests
that it contained a relic
of the True Cross.*

*Photo 24. Detail of
the inscription on
the Shrine of the
Stowe Missal, which
asks for a prayer for
Donnchadh, son of
Brian Boru.*

Most of the earlier inscriptions are in Irish, although by the fourteenth century Latin became more popular. It is interesting also that from the fourteenth century, many of the inscriptions record the names of the wives of secular patrons. There is no standard formula for these inscriptions, but typically they begin with the words 'oroit do...', that is, 'a prayer for...', followed by the names of those involved in the production of the reliquary (Photo 24). The secular patron or patrons are often placed first, the ecclesiastical patron next, followed at times by the name of the craftworker. As their primary function was to record the names of those involved in the creation or redecoration of reliquaries, they seldom refer to the contents or to the saint commemorated.

91

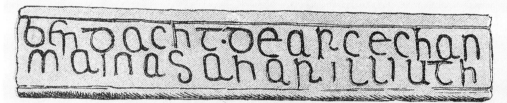

BENDACHT DE AR CECH ANMAIN AS A HARILLIUTH.

OR DO DONDCHAD MACC BRIAIN DO RIG HEREND

The importance of these inscriptions lies in the fact that they often refer to historical persons, usually kings and clerics, which enable the date and location of the shrine to be established. They are important documents in establishing who the patrons and craftworkers were and their relationship to one another. It is only through a combination of the traditional names by which reliquaries are known and historical research into the names mentioned on the inscriptions that a positive identification of reliquaries with particular saints can be made. The date of manufacture can sometimes be fixed with considerable accuracy, as in the case of the Shrine of St Lachtin's Arm, which can be dated to between the years 1118 and 1121 through the names of the Munster kings recorded on its inscription.

NAMES OF RELICS

In the historical sources written in Irish, the general term used for a relic is *mind*, which survives in modern usage as *mionn* (an oath), reflecting one of the main uses to which they were put. The word *cumdach* (a cover) is used for a reliquary, particularly for book shrines. Some relics, especially of the associative kind, were often given special names (Photo 25). In the case of bells, these were particularly numerous and largely descriptive. Some were named after the colour of their metal — *glasán* (green) and *duibhín* (black). The name *bearnán* (gapped) is associated with two bells in the British Museum — the Bearnán Conaill from Inishkeel, Co Donegal (Pl 16), and the Bearnán Cuileain from Glankeen, Co Tipperary (Pl 17). The description 'gapped' possibly relates to the fact that the bell was missing its tongue or clapper. Others were named *findfaidech* (sweet-sounding) or *ceolán* (musical), because of the sound they made. The reliquary known as the Breac Maedhóg (speckled [shrine] of St Maedhóg), associated with Drumlane, Co Cavan, was so called because it contained the relics of several people, including the martyrs Stephen, Lawrence and Clement, the ankle of St Martin and the hair of the Virgin. Many shrines are known by the term *cathach* (battler), indicating their use as talismans brought into battle to ensure victory, in the same way that in this century, icons were paraded in front of the Russian Tsar's troops before battle.

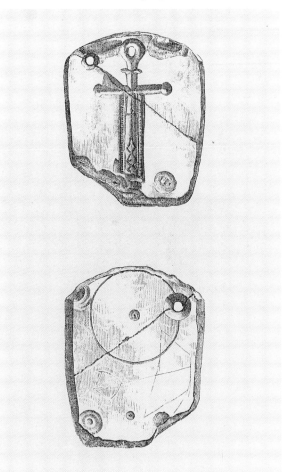

Photo 25. Stone mould, probably for casting lead badges. Popularly known as the Duibhín Déagláin, it was found in the grave of St Declan of Ardmore and was used to cure common ailments such as sore eyes and headaches.

PRESERVATION OF RELICS

Some relics and reliquaries were discovered by accident in the last few centuries. The Innisfallen Crozier was found in the River Laune near Killarney, Co Kerry, in 1867, while the Prosperous Crozier was dug out of a bog in Co Kildare in 1840. It is not known whether they were casual losses or deliberately concealed. The Shrine of the Stowe Missal (Photo 26), still containing its manuscript, was uncovered about 1735 in the walls of Lackeen Castle, Co Tipperary, while the Lismore Crozier was found behind a blocked-up doorway in Lismore Castle in 1824. Both the Stowe Missal Shrine and the Lismore Crozier were, on the evidence of their inscriptions, associated with nearby churches, and were probably hidden during periods of unrest. Perhaps the most bizarre discovery was the Irish crozier found in 1850 during the removal of a cupboard in the chambers of a London solicitor! Now in the British Museum, it is known as the Kells Crozier, although its association with the monastery of Kells, Co Meath, is uncertain.

Most reliquaries, however, were preserved above ground by their hereditary keepers, who were usually the descendants of the family of stewards or *airchinnaigh* who controlled the monastic lands. When first recorded in modern times, most of the relics had not moved very far, if at all, from where they were kept in the early Middle Ages. In some cases there is sufficient documentation to trace the families to which they belonged to medieval times. For example, the inscription on the Shrine of St Patrick's Bell, dating to *c.* AD 1100, mentions Cathalan Ua Maelchallaind (Mulholland) as the *maer* or steward of the bell. Members of the family shared the office with the O'Mellans through the Middle Ages, and some seven centuries later, in the early nineteenth century, the bell and its shrine were still in the possession of a member of the Mulholland family.

Many of the surviving reliquaries were purchased in the last century by museums or collectors, in some cases directly from their hereditary keepers. Some of the latter had fallen on hard times and parted with their heirlooms for small sums of money. The large collection of antiquities amassed by John Bell of Dungannon, Co Tyrone, was purchased by the National Museum of Scotland, Edinburgh. It included ten bells of bronze and iron provenanced to the north-east of Ireland, and these are now on long-term loan to the Ulster Museum, Belfast. Another significant group of bells and bell shrines in the collection of Thomas Cooke of Parsonstown (now Birr, Co Offaly) was purchased by the British Museum in the 1850s.

By far the greatest number, however, are preserved in the National Museum of Ireland. The collection of Irish antiquities in the National Museum has its origins in the Museum of Antiquities of the Royal Irish Academy, which began collecting on a large scale with the acquisition of the Cross of Cong in 1839 from Abbot Prendergast, the last representative of the Augustinian monks of Cong, Co Mayo.

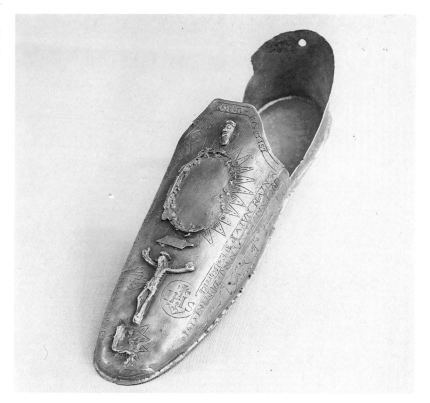

This was followed soon after with the purchase of the collections of Major Henry Sirr and Henry Dawson, Dean of St Patrick's, Dublin, the former containing the Crozier of the Abbots of Clonmacnoise. Paramount among these early collectors was the antiquary George Petrie, whose private collection included no less than six croziers, a number of bells, the Breac Maedhóg reliquary and its leather satchel (Pl 18), and the Shrine of St Brigid's Shoe (Photo 27). Petrie's collection was donated to the Museum of the Royal Irish Academy after his death in 1866. It is through the work of Petrie and his contemporaries such as John O'Donovan, Sir William Wilde and William Reeves, that we are able to identify the names of many of these objects.

New relics and reliquaries from the past are still being discovered, and research on older finds continues to add to our understanding of the role relics played in ancient Ireland. Although most are now in museums and public collections, a few are still displayed and venerated in churches close to where they were first used. In looking at them now as museum objects or works of art, their wider social, political and religious significance should never be forgotten.

FAMILIES ASSOCIATED WITH SURVIVING RELIQUARIES

Keeper	Relic	Provenance	Present location
Boland	Black Bell of St Patrick	Killower, Galway	NMI
(O, Mac) Brady	Crozier of the MacBrady's	Drumgoon, Monaghan	NMI
O'Breslen	Bearnán Conaill	Inishkeel, Donegal	BM
Deegan	Bell of St Molua	Kyle, Laois	BM
(O) Duffy	Bell of St Buodan	Culdaff, Donegal	Culdaff
(O) Farrelly	Breac Maedhóg	Drumlane, Cavan	NMI
(O) Flynn	Mias Tighearnáin	Errew, Mayo	PP
Galvin	Ardclinis Crozier	Ardclinis, Antrim	NMI
(Mac) Geoghegan	Crozier of St Columba	Durrow, Offaly	NMI
Geraghty	Black Bell of Patrick	Killower, Galway	NMI
(O) Hanley	St Berach's Crozier	Termonbarry, Roscommon	NMI
(O) Hannon	Bell of Armagh	Terryhoogan, Armagh	NMI
(O) Healy	St Lachtin's Arm	Donaghmore, Cork	NMI
(O) Heyne	Crozier of St Colman Mac Duach	Kilmacduagh, Galway	NMI
Keane	Shrine of St Senan's Bell	Scattery Is., Clare	NMI
O'Luan/Lamb	Crozier of St Dympna	Tedavnet, Monaghan	NMI
MacEnhill	Bell of Drumragh	Drumragh, Tyrone	Omagh
MacGovern	Shrine of St Maedhóg's Bell	Drumlane, Cavan	Armagh
McGurk	Bell of St Colmcille	Termonmaguirk, Tyrone	NMS
Magennis	Shrine of St Patrick's Hand	Downpatrick, Down	UM
Magroarty	Shrine of the Cathach	Ballymagroarty, Donegal	NMI
Maguire	Domhnach Airgid	Clones, Monaghan	NMI
(O) Meehan	Soiscéal Molaise	Devenish, Fermanagh	NMI
(O) Mellan	St Patrick's Bell	Armagh, Armagh	NMI
Mooney	Shrine of St Manchan	Lemanaghan, Offaly	Boher
(O) Morrisson	Shrine of the Miosach	Clonmany, Donegal	NMI
Nugent	Crozier of Fore	Fore, Westmeath	NMI
(O) Quin	Crozier of St Tola	Dysert O'Dea, Clare	NMI
(O) Reilly	St Patrick's Tooth	Killaspugbrone, Sligo	NMI
(O) Rourke	Clog na Fola	Fenagh, Leitrim	Armagh
Savage	St Patrick's Jaw	Dunturk, Down	Belfast

BM: British Museum, London
NMI: National Museum of Ireland
NMS: National Museum of Scotland
PP: Private possession
UM: Ulster Museum, Belfast

SELECT BIBLIOGRAPHY

Bourke, C. *Patrick — The Archaeology of a Saint.* HMSO, Belfast, 1993.

Crawford, H S. 'A descriptive list of Irish shrines and reliquaries', *Journal of the Royal Society of Antiquaries of Ireland,* 53, (1923), 74–93 and 151–176.

Harbison, P. *Pilgrimage in Ireland — The Monuments and the People.* Barrie & Jenkins, London, 1991.

Henry, F. *Irish Art in the Early Christian Period to AD 800.* Methuen, London, 1965.
Irish Art during the Viking Invasions, 800–1020 AD. Methuen, London, 1967.
Irish Art in the Romanesque Period, 1020–1170 AD. Methuen, London, 1970.

Lucas, A T. 'The social role of relics and reliquaries in ancient Ireland', *Journal of the Royal Society of Antiquaries of Ireland,* 116, (1986), 5–37.

Mahr, A and Raftery, J. *Christian Art in Ancient Ireland,* 2 vols. Stationery Office, Dublin, 1932 and 1941. Reprinted by A Knopf, New York, 1979.